Release

Sophia Vergez

BookLeaf
Publishing

India | USA | UK

Presentation by *BookLeaf Publishing*

Web: www.bookleafpub.com

E-mail: info@bookleafpub.com

ISBN: 9789357215237

First edition 2022

Praia de Carcavelos

1

Sprinkles of sea spray,
Salt sticks to skin
Liberated, I
Smile from within.

At Arthur's Seat:

2

I wonder,
did the many philosophers, writers and scientists
linked with this city
climb these same steps to reach
not only its heights
but their great conclusions also?

An Autumn Practice

3

My eyes track
an amber leaf
as it sashays to the ground.

Exhale. Bring
shoulders down.
Listen to the morning sounds.

I peel back
my tongue from
the roof of my mouth. Walk slow.

Autumn shows
us just how
easy it is to l e t   t   h   i   n   g   s   g
o   .   .   .

ahimsa

Am I worthy of love? I asked the Sea
How to face these fears? I asked the Sky
If I reach out and touch your kind face,
Moon, will you teach me to mirror your gentle
peace?
Softly, Wind, whisper to me...
All the ways of this delicate intimacy...

Tranquility

5

Swan swims silently
Lemon light on lake water
Hiss! Silence again.

Wombanhood

Today I started bleeding
Bright red drops on white
Granddad buys me tampons
In the middle of the night

Today I started bleeding
What a sorry sight
Blood all over car seat
Stained a rusty haematite

Today I started bleeding
I try to hide my fright
Inhale, exhale, repeat
But I cannot calm this flight

The thought you might be leaving
Chokes me up inside
I'd just accepted motherhood
Yet now I cry and hide

Tomorrow is a new day
A promise of hope
And if you can stay here, my love,
We will tread this tightrope

For all nature is balance
eart-h and h-eart are one
My womb: your first home
Yours 'til my days are done

Today I started weeping
Clear tears of relief
Joy sweeps through my body
I decline a digestif!

Home for Christmas

8

Shells crunch underfot
Icy wind whips up sea foam spray
Santa swimmers bob.

Solstice

9

Stillness of Solstice
Wind howls at the front door, sad
No leaves left to blow.

The Leaf Waltz

10

Honey, rust, cacao
Come large, come small, come them all,
Leaves dance, twirl and fall...

HNY 2023

Started twenty two babysitting two boys
chased them round gardens and played with toys
Noonie now has a boy of her own
and my bump is small, not yet fully grown
January was filled with dog walks a-plenty
Wholesome roasts and toasts to twenty
two, to friends old and new, to adventures and
and wins, to joy and a love so grand
that 50 roses don't compare to the amour
i see in your eyes and heart galore.
Vincent Van Gogh, the Nutcracker,
beaches and markets and nights ever blacker.
February saw me sending out invites
We won't mention the god-awful highlights
and the salon that shall not be named
...walking home I was so ashamed.
March we went to visit your family
and celebrated a wedding oh so happily
Cairo, Luxor, pharaohs, and mummies
temples, hot air balloons, laying on tummies
watching the sun set over the pyramids
sunrises and sunsets evermore rapid
through March - birthdays and cake
through April - Bushy park, jumps in the lake
Trying on wedding dresses and veils

Munching shakshuka in Notting Hill Gail's
In May we finally went to see Hamilton
Tried on our wedding rings, the search was won
Chopard said yes to my "happy pig" idea
Flowers surprise gifted made it a bon dia
June we took a plane and went off to France
You were Godfather and we had a good dance
I worked hard and did a stint in palliative care
Summer solstice came, I was so happy I swear
Then a phone call to say Nana was sick in July
I took annual leave to go say goodbye
The same date as her birth, she died,
It all happened so quick we cried.
Thank goodness for you, love, and days in Bath
You always stay by my side, no matter the path
Graduation ceremony, two years late
9 years after the same thing on the same date,
then psychology, now medicine, I was so proud
of friends and I, for all our work and partying
now allowed
just in time to toot two years of doctoring done
God it was hard but that night we had some fun
August already and the wedding is almost here
not everyone can come, including some dear,
floral crowns and opera at my Surrey Hen party
Nappies and cake at Noonie's baby shower,
sparkly
times approaching as we travel back to France

In September to dance, and say "I do" to this
romance
October rolled round, another baby born
Winkworth arboretum in Autumn colours
adorned
Headed into November with a new job
And started growing our own little blob! :-)
December was filled with the usual carols and
cheer
And finished as we sang out HAPPY NEW
YEAR!

PEACE

I daydream so loudly
Get lost in my own mind
Until I lose sight and forget
that I can actually find
peace and anchoring
anywhere, anytime
one breath - a lifeline.

Resolutions and Blooming

15

After pandemics and lockdowns
I think we are all so very tired
of the new year new me trope
I hope
that this year I am kind,
start slow, and rest in the
gentleness of January
Just as the roots gather food
deep down below the earth
yet leave only stillness of branches
for us to see up above
I will be planting my intentions
and gathering strength
from a place of stillness and
calm. Ready to bloom in Spring.

Strikes

I want a strike where we all walk out
of less-than healthcare
of services that can't achieve
of a world where MP's watch us suffer on our
knees
whilst they host parties to drink wine and eat
cheese
why are we so scrutinised by the likes of the
GMC?
when they are so incompetent and the whole
world can see
We work hard because we love to care
but ignoring our pleas, oh how they dare
I want a strike where the MP's walk out
And we all walk into a better world, no doubt.

Medicine

I sit and prescribe more pills for more ills
than I care to count
I am beginning to realise
that we are only healing the havoc
we created in the first place

the singing crystal feels more like healing
sound, its own medicine
perhaps i can be a medicine woman
after all

Alone and not lonely

18

another year gone
and I've fallen more deeply
in love with, yes, me.

My Frenchie

You're the gin to my tonic, the poet to my pen
the moon to my stars, et le coq to my hen
I couldn't have chosen a better mari
to love and to honour pour toute ma vie

The Touchstones

The Touchstones stand silent as Fire rages
thereon
Smoke rises as Sun taught her for centuries gone
The Moon moves Tides, but they ebb and flow
Destruction by Humans? - of this, they know...

As Seagulls swoop and cry, my tears fly to wind
Kids run past Trees, unaware and bare-limbed
This morning the radio said forty degrees
Stony look on Stone's face, no sign of unease

What must they have seen, whilst stationed
here? I ask
Is it too late or too great, this most urgent of
tasks?
Will we miss the mystic moment, too busy, too
rushed
to hear Earth's voice, so quiet and hushed?

As Sun, as Smoke, now Temperature rises,
violent.
The Touchstones stand silent.

An ode to little fig

21

I promise to love
You unconditionally
with all that I am.